Assessment of Social and Emotional Skills in the OECD's SSES Study

Dr. Milos Kankaras

Published by Dr. Milos Kankaras, 2023.

ASSESSMENT OF SOCIAL AND EMOTIONAL SKILLS IN THE OECD'S SSES STUDY

First edition. November 5, 2023.

Copyright © 2023 Dr. Milos Kankaras.

ISBN: 979-8223022886

Written by Dr. Milos Kankaras.

Table of Contents

Assessment of Social and Emotional Skills in the OECD's SSES Study. 1

Introduction 2

1. OECD's Survey on Social and Emotional Skills (SSES) 4

1. General outline of the scale development process 16

2. Development of an initial item pool 19

3. Translatability analysis 22

4. Cognitive interviews 24

5. Study with parent-report scales 29

6. Item Trials 33

7. Field Test 43

8. Main Study 53

9. How to use SSES assessment scales 57

10. Concluding discussion 62

References 64

Annex: SSES Assessment Scales 68

Assessment of Social and Emotional Skills in the OECD's SSES Study

Introduction

In the world of educational and psychological assessment, few endeavors are as challenging or as rewarding as the development of instruments that accurately measure social and emotional skills. The OECD's Study on Social and Emotional Skills (SSES) represents a monumental step in this field, with the creation of the SSES Inventory – an instrument crafted through a global, multidisciplinary effort. This manuscript delves into the intricate process and the significant outcomes of this landmark study, as detailed in the comprehensive account of its development.

At the heart of the SSES study lies a rigorous instrument development process, tailored to assess 15 social and emotional skills across 45 scales. This expansive project marshaled the collective expertise of 15 international research teams and engaged more than 150,000 participants—students, parents, and teachers. Its reach spanned eleven cities globally, underscoring the universal importance of these skills. With the coordination of over a thousand professionals, including project managers, researchers, translators, and data analysts, the process was a mosaic of cultural and methodological diversity, aiming for an assessment tool of unparalleled scope and precision.

Initially grappling with 380 assessment items, the teams' methodical analysis and meticulous refinement culminated in the selection of the most robust 120 items, some unaltered and others slightly adapted. The multi-faceted approach merged quantitative and qualitative research methodologies, yielding a harmonious synthesis of data and insights. This approach ensured that the resulting scales were not only reliable and valid but also resonant across different cultures, languages, and educational contexts.

The book sheds light on the SSES Inventory's performance along the various stages of its empirical testing. The instrument demonstrated remarkable versatility, adapting to the developmental stages of students beginning from the age of ten. One of the key highlights was the Inventory's triangulated approach, utilizing feedback from students, parents, and teachers to enrich the data and enhance scale validity.

As Kankaraš et al. (2019) indicate, the triangulation not only solidifies the SSES Inventory as a multifaceted measure but also underscores the value of gathering diverse perspectives. The Inventory's structure allows for the application within individual respondent groups, yet the most comprehensive picture emerges when the scales are administered collectively to students, parents, and teachers.

The book concludes by emphasizing the SSES Inventory's significance as a psychometrically sound tool for measuring the social and emotional skills of youths aged 10 to 18. The study's implications extend far beyond the academic domain, signaling potential applications in policy-making, educational interventions, and cross-cultural understandings of student development. The SSES Inventory stands as a testament to the collaborative spirit of international research and the pursuit of nuanced, culturally competent assessment methods in the evolving landscape of social and emotional learning.

1. OECD's Survey on Social and Emotional Skills (SSES)

Social and emotional skills are seen as the key components of 21st-century skills due to their critical role in an individual's personal and career development, and positive societal functioning (National Academy of Sciences, 2012; De Fruyt, Wille and John, 2015; Trilling and Fadel, 2009). A growing realization of the importance of social and emotional skills has led to increased attention to this topic among researchers, policy-makers and practitioners. OECD studies such as the Programme for International Student Assessment (PISA) and the Survey of Adult Skills (PIAAC) primarily focus on cognitive skills, such as reading/literacy and mathematics/numeracy. However, in recent years, PISA has broadened its scope by assessing a growing set of social and emotional skills, such as academic self-efficacy, perseverance, openness to knowledge, and intellectual curiosity. The OECD has taken this work further with the development of a new Study on Social and Emotional Skills (SSES), a comprehensive international assessment of the social and emotional skills of school-age children.

The OECD initiated the Study on Social and Emotional Skills (SSES) in 2016 to gather empirical evidence on the social and emotional skills of young people in school and the factors that influence their development. The overall purpose of the Study on Social and Emotional Skills is to assist participating cities and countries to understand the importance of these skills better and to improve policy measures for the development of social and emotional skills of their students.

The main goals of the SSES are twofold. First, it aims to provide policy-makers and educators with information about the conditions and practices that foster or hinder the development of students' social and emotional skills in schools, at home, in local communities, and in societies as a whole. Its second objective is to explore the relevance of different social and emotional skills on a broad range of life events and outcomes in areas of education, health, civic participation, and overall personal well-being.

The SSES study is complex and ground-breaking, involving tens of thousands of students, parents and teachers from all around the world, and gathers information on a broad set of personal and contextual factors. This section briefly outlines the study's main aspects.

1.1 Social and emotional skills assessed in the study

The SSES assesses the following 15 social and emotional skills of students grouped into five broader skill domains (Chernyshenko, Kankaraš, and Drasgow, 2019):

- Task Performance: 1. Self-Control; 2. Responsibility; 3. Persistence
- Emotional Regulation: 4. Stress Resistance; 5. Emotional Control; 6. Optimism
- Engaging with Others: 7. Energy; 8. Assertiveness; 9. Sociability
- Open-Mindedness: 10. Curiosity; 11. Creativity; 12. Tolerance
- Collaboration: 13. Empathy; 14. Co-operation; 15. Trust

The study also includes two additional skills that are assessed in the form of indices calculated from a selection of items that belong to scales of other related skills:

- Skills estimated from indices: Self-Efficacy; Achievement Motivation.

1.2 Contextual information collected in the study

Apart from assessing students' social and emotional skills, the study examines a broad scope of contextual factors, including students' socio-demographic background, family, peer, school and wider community environment (Kankaraš & Suarez-Alvarez, 2019). Collecting contextual information is critical in helping to understand how students' social and emotional skills have developed and how these skills may be improved. Students learn in many different settings, including in their families, schools and communities, with each context playing an essential role throughout childhood and adolescence. Contextual information gives us a better understanding of what helps and what hinders social and emotional skills development, including the policies and practices that support them.

1.3 Study respondents

The study assesses the social and emotional skills of two groups (cohorts) of students:

- 10-year-olds (younger cohort)
- 15-year-olds (older cohort)

The study also collects data from three additional groups of respondents: students' parents, teachers (who know selected students best) and school principals.

1.4 Participating cities

Ten cities from nine countries have participated in the first round of the SSES are Bogota and Manizales (Colombia), Daegu (South Korea), Helsinki (Finland), Houston (USA), Istanbul (Turkey), Moscow (Russia), Ottawa (Canada), Sintra (Portugal) and Suzhou (China).

1.5 Study timeline

Initial preparations for the study started at the end of 2016, with instrument development and survey preparation work being conducted between 2017 and 2019. The Main Study is administered in October and November 2019. An international report with the main findings was published in December 2020.

In this book, we will describe the SSES assessment scales and the process of their development.

1.6 The SSES assessment approach

There is a long tradition of measuring social and emotional skills both in academic and applied settings, and a wide range of instruments and assessment techniques have been developed for these purposes. Many different measurement approaches are used to assess social and emotional skills, including self-reports, reports from others, such as peers, teachers and parents, behavioral observations, performance tasks, biographical data, projective tests, situational judgment tests and think-aloud protocols (Kankaraš M. , 2017).

We chose to develop scales in the form of self- and others-reports as the best suited for the SSES. This form of scale allowed for fast and efficient administration with a large number of respondents in both school (students and teachers) and home (parents) settings. Due to the speed of their administration (around 1 minute per skill scale), they enable us to assess a broad set of student's social and emotional skills while at the same time still obtaining satisfactory psychometric characteristics. These scales tend to produce consistent results, and in many cases, provide a remarkably good approximation of objective measures (Duckworth, Tsukayama, & May, 2010; Connelly & Ones, 2010). Moreover, a considerable body of literature in the social sciences indicates that people generally react reasonably well to questionnaires and can generally describe their typical behavior in the intended way (Krosnick, 1999; Heine, Buchtel, & Norenzayan, 2008).

Furthermore, the fact that these types of scales were by far the most used for assessment of these psychological characteristics meant that we do not have to start constructing the instruments from scratch but can instead build upon many existing measures. Importantly, these scales have been used internationally, with many translated versions used in different cultures worldwide. These scales have also been used both with school-aged children and adults, thus allowing us to gain a better insight into the age-appropriateness of scale content to our target population of students.

The use of scales in the form of self- and others-reports also allowed us the possibility to implement the triangulation approach. Triangulation of assessment scales implies obtaining reports on students not only from students themselves but also from their parents and teachers. Triangulation of assessment scales enables us to mutually validate reports from the three groups of informers on students' social and emotional skills, and as such, substantially improves the validity of self- and other-reports (Kankaraš et al., 2019). Although triangulation can be attempted with various forms of assessment approaches, it is usually prohibitively expensive and thus rarely used. However, the high efficiency and ease of administration of the self- and other-report scales meant that it could be applied in the SSES, while still keeping the overall costs relatively low.

Constrains of self- and others-reports

One of the main constrains of the self- and others-report scales is that respondents may misinterpret the questions in several ways. Students, parents and teachers are also not equally reliable reporters of students' inner states, such as feelings or self-perceptions. They might also have difficulty in retrieving the required information, in which case they might resort to provide a socially desirable answer. Even when they are motivated and interpret the question correctly, they may be suspectable to various memory biases and inconsistencies.

Social desirability is another threat to the validity of self-reports. Furthermore, whenever the so-called rating scales are used (i.e., where respondents are asked to rate a particular statement, mostly using five answer options ranging from "strongly agree" to "strongly disagree"), responses are subject to various response-style biases. The most ubiquitous among these is an "acquiescence" response style – the tendency to agree with statements irrespective of their content.

Another validity threat to both self-reports is the so-called "reference bias," i.e., a situation in which people from different countries answer the same question using different standards or reference systems. For example, a question such as: "I treat others with respect" (a question from the SSES' cooperation scale) may be answered differently depending on a persons' view of what it means in a given culture (i.e., reference point) to treat others with respect.

One of the critical issues for the SSES study is the ability of younger students to provide valid and reliable information on their typical behaviors, thoughts and feelings. This is why the age of our younger cohort was determined following previous research that has established that students' self-reports on personality and social and emotional skills can be used from the age of 10 onwards (Soto, John, Gosling, & Potter, 2011). This capacity is dependent on a series of critical factors, including language proficiency, but also cognitive and social development (John & De Fruyt, 2015). First, children need to have acquired a certain vocabulary and a basic reading level to be able to administer the assessment. This is why simplicity and clarity of used language is a critical requirement for assessment items. These constraints require grammatically streamlined and short items, an easily understandable response scale format, and clear instructions.

1.6.1 Triangulation of data on students' social and emotional skills

The triangulation of students' socio-emotional skills assessment is a critical assessment aspect of the SSES (Kankaraš, Feron, & Renbarger, 2019). First, the assessment through parents and teachers increases the content validity of the estimates of students' socio-emotional skills by providing information on students' behaviors across different contexts. Research shows that all perspectives have unique and valuable viewpoints on individual differences, with reports correlating with one another between 0.30 – 0.60 (John & De Fruyt, 2015). The magnitude of these correlations suggests that all perspectives share some variance but also have their own specific and informative viewpoint. This is a critical aspect as students may behave differently in different settings and choosing information from any of those settings may provide a somewhat biased representation of students' social and emotional skills. The opportunity to combine information on students' skills from personal, school and family perspectives yields a better representation and understanding of students' behaviors in the most essential contexts that affect school-age students. Likewise, obtaining information from other sources that know the student well permits controlling for various sources of measurement error presented in self-reports, such as social desirability or unrealistic self-perceptions.

Parents are valuable sources of information on typical behaviors, thoughts and feelings of their children, especially at a younger age. They have long-term and close relationships with their children, have seen them grow and develop, and know first-hand their life situation, personal preferences and practices. Teachers' reports are also highly valuable because they have much experience dealing with many children and can evaluate students' social and emotional skills as reasonably objective non-family members. Furthermore, teachers have experience with children in a more structured classroom context and are in a good position to observe more interpersonal and task-oriented skills. In contrast, parents provide ratings relying on the home context (John & De Fruyt, 2015).[1]

1.6.2 Short rating scales

In large-scale surveys, existing instruments designed for assessing social and emotional skills are often too long to use. Over the past few decades, studies have tried to shorten the length of instruments with varied success. Shorter scales reduce respondent burden and improve engagement, which can increase the quality of answers. Although most of the psychometric characteristics of short scales are inferior to longer scales, short scales can reach comparable levels of criterion validity as longer scales measuring the same construct (Burisch, 1984; Robins, Hendin, & Trzesniewski, 2001; Thalmayer, Saucier, & Eigenhuis, 2011). Other studies have shown that short scales have satisfactory test-retest reliability and convergence validity (Gosling, Rentfrow, & Swann, 2003; Robins, Hendin, & Trzesniewski, 2001).

Moreover, shorter and quicker assessments make them more cost-effective and leave more room to assess other relevant concepts and contextual factors, thus enriching the overall analytical potential of a study. On the negative side, the use of short scales tends to lead to increased measurement error and, consequently, lower scale reliability (Kankaraš M., 2017). Also, fewer items mean fewer aspects of a measured construct can be assessed, reducing content validity. Finally, when measures only have one or two items per scale, they cannot be used to identify underlying or statistically latent scale structures. This has both methodological and substantive consequences and can affect the study's aim to assess latent constructs that cannot be measured directly.

Therefore, the SSES attempts to use the smallest number of questions for assessing each of the selected social and emotional skills, while still ensuring satisfactory levels of reliability, validity and comparability of obtained skill estimates. An extensive instrument development process was used to select the best items that provide the most information per unit of response time.

1.6.3 Scale comparability

How we can compare information on social and emotional skills depends on how equivalent the scales are across different groups. Ideally, the scales would be equivalent across gender, cohort and sites. However, when the scales are not equivalent (measurement non-invariance), this suggests that the construct that we measure has a different structure or a different meaning to different groups. If that is the case, we cannot meaningfully compare the construct across the different groups. However, comparability of constructs across different population groups is a matter of degree, with different levels of achieved comparability possible (Kankaraš M. , 2010).

This is why comparability (measurement invariance) is tested in steps, across different levels. The analysis starts from the lowest level of comparability expressed in configural invariance (invariance of the model form), through metric invariance (invariance of relationship parameters) and finishing with scalar invariance (invariance of group averages) as the highest level of comparability. Configural invariance is the least strict and means that the structure of the construct is the same across groups, but not its meaning. Metric equivalence means that the construct has the same meaning across groups, but it does not guarantee that other factors that vary across groups are not involved. Scalar equivalence indicates that the construct not only has the same meaning across the groups but also that influence of other factors is the same across groups. Metric equivalence is needed to compare the strengths of relationships between variables across groups while scalar equivalence allows for comparisons of group averages.

There is extensive evidence that the selected social and emotional skills are conceptually comparable across cultures; countries and economies for both adults and children from different cultural backgrounds (Paunonen et al., 1996; McCrae and Costa Jr., 1997; Schmitt et al., 2007; McCrae and Terracciano, 2005; Tackett et al., 2012. However, there is also evidence that a simple comparison of scale scores across cultures may not work due to possible method bias resulting from cultural differences in the interpretation of questions. Therefore, method bias stemming from social desirability, response styles and the meaning of particular words received particular scrutiny in the SSES. In order to improve cross-cultural comparability of the assessment scales as much as possible, the OECD has worked with leading experts in the field to develop comprehensive methodological, translation and statistical procedures that minimize the possibility of method biases.

1.7 Innovative assessment design elements

In order to deal with some of the potential issues of self- and others-reports, several relatively new assessment approaches were introduced in the SSES. These innovative assessment designs are intended to complement self- and others-report scales, further improving their psychometric qualities.

1.7.1 Anchoring vignettes

The SSES includes anchoring vignettes in order to enhance the cross-country comparability of the results. Reference bias refers to a situation in which people from different countries answer the same question using different reference standards. Reference bias is problematic when comparing aggregate data between cultures, but less so when comparing individual scores within the same culture. Anchoring vignettes are sets of questions specially designed to account for reference bias. They are designed to identify the reference system respondents use for evaluating behaviors presented in a given scale. Based on the answers obtained from anchoring vignettes, respondents' answers to assessment scales are adjusted to account for differences in their reference systems. This adjustment could reduce possible bias introduced by respondents from different cultures using different reference systems for evaluating the same behaviors.

In order to be able to control for possible effects of the reference bias, a new set of anchoring vignettes was developed for initial testing in the SSES. For each of the five broad skill domains, a set of three anchoring vignettes were designed, depicting behaviors of a person with the high, medium and low level of skills from a given domain. Thus, an entire set of 15 anchoring vignettes was developed and used in the Main Study.

1.7.2 Behavioral indicators

Gathering information on how students behave – or manifest their social and emotional skills – is a useful addition to the student, parent and teacher reports on these skills. Behavioral indicators represent a set of questions on students' behaviors at home or in class/school that correspond to selected social and emotional skills, i.e., that can be seen as a concrete manifestation of these skills. Examples of such behaviors are school absenteeism, class disruption behaviors, health-related behaviors, etc.

1.7.3 Controlling for acquiescence response style

We mentioned that the "acquiescence" response style – the tendency to agree with statements irrespective of their content – is one of the typical threats to self- and others-reports (Rammstedt, Goldberg, & Borg, 2010; Rammstedt & Kemper, 2011). One way to control the acquiescence response style is by using both positively and negatively worded statements in an instrument so that the effects of the agreeing tendency can be identified and controlled.

In some cases, the number of positively and negatively worded items in a scale is kept the same in order to achieve full balance out over the scale. However, negatively worded items are often harder to understand, have higher cognitive load and response times, and are more sensitive to differences in educational and socio-economic backgrounds in respondents. This is why they tend to lead to scales with lower precision and internal consistency.

Thus, there is a trade-off between the scales' psychometric quality and its ability to detect and control for acquiescence response bias. In the SSES, this trade-off was handled by ensuring that each final scale had at least one negatively formulated item, but the scales were not required to have an equal number of these items across scales. Instead, their final number in a scale depended on their psychometric quality.

1. General outline of the scale development process

———

A ssessment scales measuring selected social and emotional skills needed to be developed for the study. In consultation with experts from our Technical Advisory Group (TAG)[2], we decided to implement a triangulation assessment approach in which we assess students' skills not only through their self-reports but also through reports of their parents and teachers. This tasked us with the development of 15 assessment scales, appropriate for use by four target respondent groups (10- and 15-year-old students, their parents and their teachers). In addition, each of these 15 scales had to be translated into 11 languages and verified for application in 10 cities around the world.

In light of the complexity of the tasks, the instrument development process was long, comprehensive and elaborate, including a multitude of rounds of quantitative and qualitative empirical testing. With five empirical rounds and the participation of more than 150 thousand respondents worldwide, it is one of the largest instrument development processes undertaken in this area.

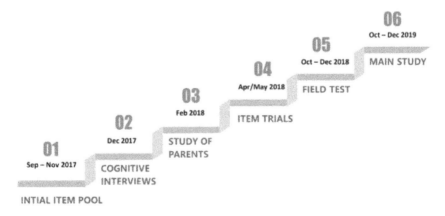

06 Oct – Dec 2019 MAIN STUDY

05 Oct – Dec 2018 FIELD TEST

04 Apr/May 2018 ITEM TRIALS

03 Feb 2018 STUDY OF PARENTS

02 Dec 2017 COGNITIVE INTERVIEWS

01 Sep – Nov 2017 INTIAL ITEM POOL

The assessment instruments' development process started with the creation of an initial item bank of 20 items per skill (or in total 20 items x 19 skills = 380 items). Although the target number of social and emotional skills to be assessed in the SSES was 15, we have initially started with the development of 19 skill scales. This was done in order to use empirical data gathered from the initial phases of empirical testing to determine which 15 scales are functioning the best. The final selection of 15 social and emotional skills to be assessed in the Main Study of the SSES was made after the Field Test.

Assessment instruments in the study are divided into two broad groups: self-reports and others-reports. The self-report scales ask students to report on their own behavior, thoughts and feelings. In others-reports scales, parents and teachers are asked to report on students' behaviors, thoughts and feelings. For better inter-comparability of the self- and others-reports, the same items are used in both types of instruments. However, the number of items per scale varied depending on the respondents[3].

While students and parents provide a report on one student, teachers often report on multiple students. This is why assessment scales for teachers are kept as brief as possible in order to lower their response burden. The instrument development process for students', parents' and teachers'-reports, including the number of items in each of the phases, is outlined in Table 1.

Table 1. Development of the SSES assessment scales

Study stage	Timeline	Items per skill				Number of skills
		Older cohort	Younger cohort	Parents	Teachers	Both cohorts
Initial item pool	Sep-Nov 2017	20	20			19
TAG evaluation	Dec 2017	15	12			19
Translatability assessment	Dec 2017	15	12	15	15	19
Cognitive interviews	Dec 2017		12			19
Online study of parents	Feb 2018			10		19
Item Trials	Apr 2018	15	10	10	10	19
Field Test	Oct/Nov 2018	10	8	8	3	19
Main Study	Oct/Nov 2019	8	8	8	3	15
Total number of items		120	120	120	45	

Note: TAG - Technical Advisory Group.

Anchoring Vignettes

The same 15 anchoring vignettes are included in all three respondents' questionnaires: student, parent and teacher. They were first tested on students in both cohorts during the Item Trials. Based on the Item Trials findings, anchoring vignettes were modified and prepared for the Field Test. After further adjustments, they were implemented in the Main Study as part of students', parents' and teachers' questionnaires.

The instrument development process started in September 2017 with the development of the initial item pool. It then went through a number of phases, using varying methodological approaches until their application in the Main Study in October-November 2019. In the following sections, we will illustrate in more detail each of the phases of the instrument development of the SSES assessment scales before focusing on the results from the Main Study and the final forms of the assessment scales.

2. Development of an initial item pool

———

T he development of the SSES assessment scales started with creating an initial item pool of 20 items per skill scale, i.e., 380 assessment items (20 items x 19 skills). Construction of the initial item pool was based on the following principles:

- Priority is given to already used and empirically verified items
- Priority is given to items in the public domain
- Items should have been used with students of both age groups
- Item formulations should be as clear and concise as possible
- Preference is given to items with a Likert-type response format
- Preference is given to items used in instruments applied internationally
- Preference is given to items that apply to all three respondent groups: students, parents and teachers

We wanted to make the best use of the substantial empirical work done in this area before. Most of the selected 19 skills have been investigated throughout decades of empirical research in both academic and practice settings. Thus, it was essential to use the resulting body of knowledge, both in terms of assessment instruments and accompanying theoretical frameworks and empirical results. Building our scales based on existing instruments would not only make our task more manageable and our instruments psychometrically sounder. It would also allow for more comparability between the new SSES findings and previous research in the area of social and emotional skills. In such a way, we could interpret obtained results in a broader context of previous empirical research, thus reaching more insightful policy conclusions.

We also decided against using any copyrighted assessment materials due to our desire to make the final versions of the SSES instruments publicly available to all researchers and practitioners. We also prioritized the use of scales and items that were used across a wider age range in early teens and adolescence, in line with the age of our two target populations.

In order for items to be comparable across the three groups of respondents, items should as much as possible focus on observable behaviors as indicators of social and emotional skills (Varni, et al., 2015). At the same time, it was inevitable also to include assessment items that require self-reflection, as these are necessary in assessment some social and emotional skills, such as those related to emotional regulation. Question wording, syntax and semantics have been kept as simple as possible to improve understanding and minimize the cognitive burden.

The majority of items in the initial item pool were selected from the International Personality Item Pool (IPIP[4]) database. The IPIP database consists of more than 3 000 assessment items belonging to more than 250 scales designed and used for the assessment of different personality characteristics. Items from several other existing scales of social and emotional skills were used as well. Finally, in scales where not enough appropriate existing items existed, new items were drafted in the same format and style of the items obtained from existing scales.

After construction of the initial item pool, items were evaluated by a group of experts from the Technical Advisory Group (TAG) based on the following set of criteria:

- Conceptual overlap with own scale (should be as high as possible: convergent validity)
- Conceptual overlap with other scales (should be as low as possible: divergent validity)
- Clarity/cognitive burden

- Word appropriateness (e.g., presence of idioms)
- Appropriateness for 10-year-olds
- Content validity (covers all relevant aspects of a skill)
- Cross-cultural appropriateness

Based on TAG feedback, the item bank was then reduced to 15 and 12 items per skill for the older and younger cohorts, respectively. TAG feedback is also used to modify some of the remaining items further to simplify their wording and sentence structure and make them more accessible to students of the younger cohort.

3. Translatability analysis

A fter constructing the initial item pool in the English source language, an evaluation of their translatability into other languages was conducted. The objective of this phase was to investigate to which degree the English-language formulations of selected assessment items are translatable into other languages. Identifying any translatability issues at this stage would allow us to modify item wordings in the source language. In this way, we could prevent problems in the translation process and cross-cultural comparability of items at the later stages.

The translatability analysis was conducted by cApStAn, one of the members of the SSES consortium. For this assessment, three linguists were asked to evaluate the translatability of selected assessment items into the following languages: Russian, Turkish and Spanish (Latin American). These languages were selected for two reasons. First, they were the languages of some of our survey participants and, as such, the target languages of our future translation process. Secondly, each of these languages belonged to different language families (Sloven, Turkic and Roman language families respectively) and differed from the language family of English as the source language (German language family). This diversity of languages was a critical point in the process of translatability assessment as it enables a broader evaluation of the presence of translation issues into different languages.

The linguists produced draft translations of the statements in the first person singular for all 285 assessment items (15 items x 19 scales). Their translations were not intended for further use, but to help them identify and describe the potential issues future translators might encounter, for the statements in the third-person singular, general comments concerning the double-gender issue was made. In a few cases, specific comments were also annotated.

A set of 14 translatability categories is used to label the potential translation, adaptation and cultural issues identified and described in their comments. These included whether the question was straightforward, had known difficulty, was potentially ambiguous, was unnecessarily complex, had potential cultural issues, was inconsistent, had logical problems, etc.

Whenever possible, the linguists produce a translation note that can be inserted to clarify a given term or expression or to indicate the type of adaptation that may be necessary. In some cases, alternative wording is also proposed. This new formulation suggests a way to circumvent the problem (without losing meaning).

Once the three linguists provided their translatability assessments, a senior linguist at cApStAn collated and consolidated their more relevant comments and integrated them with additional remarks and solutions. The full report was then returned to the OECD for consideration and further processing.

The translatability analysis provided useful information and allowed for the early identification of several potential wording and translation issues. Based on this report, several items were slightly adjusted to more optimal forms for future translations. Importantly, the full report, with notes for each assessment item and suggestions for its adaptation and translation was made available and used by all translators in future translation rounds (before Item Trials, Field Test and Main Study).

4. Cognitive interviews

―――

Once 12 items per scale for younger cohort students were determined, they were used in the next phase of the instrument development process – the Cognitive Interviews. The focus of this phase was to investigate the degree to which students understand selected assessment items. Given that one of the main concerns of the instrument development process was the appropriateness of the instruments to the 10-year-olds, it was decided that the entire sample of students for Cognitive Interviews is from the student population of the younger cohort. For the same reason, although we were dealing with a convenience sample, an effort was made to over-sample a disproportionate number of minority students and students from disadvantaged backgrounds.

5.1 Overview of the research stage: Cognitive Interviews

5.1.1 Research objective:

Examination of students' correct understanding and appropriateness of assessment items and response scales to identify problematic items (words or formulations) and take appropriate remedial actions.

5.1.2 Participants

A total of 37 interviews were completed with children ages 10-11 from the USA (all from Columbus, Ohio metro area). Of the participants, 24 (64.9%) were male and 13 (35.1%) were female. Participants self-identified as White/Caucasian (48.6%), Black/African/

African-American (37.8%), mixed-race (10.8%), and Native American (2.7%).

5.1.3 Materials

Two hundred twenty-eight assessment items (12 items per 19 scales) selected for administration with the younger cohort were used in this phase. In order to reduce the response burden of young students, the item pool of 228 items was divided into ten forms, with each form consisting of two full assessment scales, i.e., 24 items (two forms were partially overlapping). This meant that each question stem was evaluated by about four students, while all participating students evaluated response scales.

5.1.4 Method

Semi-structured interviews were used, with investigators interviewing each child separately. Interviews lasted around 30 minutes. The interview protocol consisted of four parts. Firstly, after giving introductory explanations to a student, investigators were instructing them to read the list of 24 questions and accompanying answer options. Students were then asked a few general questions about the questions as a whole (e.g., "Did you find the questions easy to read?" and "Were there any words that you did not understand?"). The interviewers were then going through each of the assessment questions separately and after reading them aloud, asking the students, "What did the question make you think about?". Finally, in the last stage, the interviewers were asking students five questions about the 5-point Likert agree/disagree scale (e.g., "What does strongly disagree mean to you?"). Throughout the interview, whenever a student's response was indicating that he or she has an issue with a particular question or a word in a question, the interviewer was asking a follow-up question to find the root cause of the problem that the students had with a given assessment item.

5.2 Main findings

5.2.1 Assessment items

Participants generally found most of the statements easy to read and comprehend. Out of the 888 times, students read assessment questions (24 questions for 37 students), in 85% of cases, students did not report any issues in understanding or wording of a given question. However, given that four students evaluated each question, a broader proportion of items – 41% of them – was flagged by at least one of the four students.

Most of the flagged questions had only one of four students having some issue with the wording or a particular word, although there were a few dozen of the items that were found problematic by multiple students. Most participants had a few words they did not understand, and many had statements they struggled to understand, even if they knew all the words in the sentence.

Some participants found a lack of context for some statements problematic. A few would ask for clarification from the interviewer, such as whether they should answer "for school or at home." Additionally, for some participants, statement phrasing and structure were challenging (e.g., with the item structure from the BFI2 inventory, e.g., "I am inventive, find clever ways to do things").

5.2.2 Response options

In general, participants had an easy time choosing their answers. When they indicated it was difficult to choose an answer, the reasoning varied but was often due to their need for time to think about their response.

The other common reason was an admitted lack of understanding of the whole statement or just part of it. Participants did not have much feedback on the appearance of the response options, though a few mentioned they liked having both a number and text for each choice. Except for two participants, all others comfortable with the five-point scale and provided appropriate answers for the meaning of each response option.

5.3 Use of research findings

Findings from the cognitive interviews were used to re-evaluate each of the 228 items with the dual goal:

- To identify from each of the 12-item scales two items that will be excluded from scales for younger-cohort in the further process of instrument development
- To account for each of the observed issues that students have reported by making necessary adjustments, if appropriate.
- Revision work was conducted by a team of psychometricians and researchers from the OECD and the Drasgow Psychometric Group. The main principles used to exclude those items were:
- Found to be problematic by multiple students;
- Much of the item stem is problematic;
- Do not provide an easy way to fix the identified issue;

Based on these principles, two items were excluded from the 19 scales for the younger cohort. The remaining flagged items (55 of them) had fewer identified problems, with the only issue in many of them being one less frequent word. In such cases, the word is then changed into a more common word (e.g., changing the flagged word "error" into "mistake" or "anticipate" into "predict"). In a few other cases, a small part of question formulation was simplified (e.g., "I tend to believe" into "I believe").

Also, in some cases, a more complex wording structure was simplified. For example, question stem "I am inventive, I find clever ways to do things" was changed into "I find new ways to do things," while question stem "I avoid working hard when possible" was changed into "I don't like working hard."

Overall, the findings of the Cognitive Interviews with 10-year-old students were instrumental in identifying potentially problematic questions and more difficult words, especially for the younger cohort and students from disadvantaged backgrounds. These findings helped select the best items for the next phases of instrument development but also allowed for improvements to a substantial set of items used in assessment scales in all three groups of respondents (students, teachers, and parents).

5. Study with parent-report scales

—

After obtaining initial information on the quality and appropriateness of assessment scales from the Cognitive Interviews with students, we wanted to do the first test of the functioning of the parent-reports, before they are to be used in the Item Trials. We conducted an online study with parents' and teachers' assessment scales in February 2018, with a sample of more than 1,000 parents from the United States. In this study, assessment instruments consisted of those ten items per skill that were selected for use in self-reports of both younger and older cohorts after the Cognitive Interviews.

6.1 Overview of the research stage: Study with parent-report scales

6.1.1 Research objectives:

The primary purpose of this study was to explore the measurement properties of the 19 scales and each of the 190 assessment items, including their relations with other relevant variables. The second goal was to test new questions from the newly developed contextual questionnaire for parents. Finally, we also wanted to get the first indication of the timing needed to complete these scales by parents.

6.1.2 Participants

A total of 1070 complete and validated questionnaires were obtained from a sample of parents, which were at the time living in the USA. Respondents were paid for participation and were sampled through invitations from an online panel based on their children's age (only those between ages 9 – 16 were allowed to participate). Respondents' ages varied between 27 and 64; 79% of mothers and 21% of fathers were in the sample of parents.

6.1.3 Materials and method

All 19 assessment scales, each consisting of 10 questions, were administered. The items/questions were formulated as others-reports. Also, a contextual questionnaire with around 100 additional questions on parents' socio-demographic characteristics, home activities, parental styles, attitudes and skills, child's wellbeing indicators, characteristics of their child, as well as a set of behavioral indicators, was included.

Questionnaires were administered online with an average administration time of around 25 minutes.

6.2 Main findings

The assessment scales were evaluated in terms of reliability and validity. Reliability coefficients indicate the degree to which a scale consistently measures a given construct, i.e., whether the items in the scale reflect the same underlying construct. Validity refers to whether a scale measures the skill they are supposed to measure. We evaluate this by observing whether the scale is related to the measures of the same skill (convergent validity) and whether the scale is not related to measures of different skills (divergent validity). Validity is also examined by analyzing the relationships between the scale and criterion/outcome variables, such as the relationship between skill scales and students' educational achievement (i.e., criterion/predictive validity).

6.2.1 Scale reliability

Reliabilities of the assessment scales were satisfactory, averaging at 0.83 and varying between 0.74 (Energy) and 0.93 (Persistence), except for the scale assessing Critical Thinking (α=0.55, see Figure 1).

Figure 1. Reliability of students' social and emotional skill scales

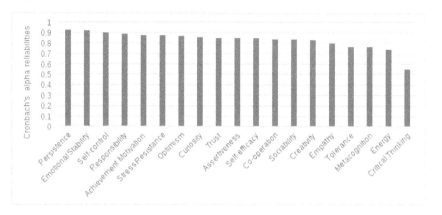

6.2.2 Validity of assessment scales

In terms of the convergent and divergent validities of the scales, scales showed mixed results, with somewhat inflated inter-correlations with corresponding scales from the same skill domain as well as with the non-corresponding scales from other skill domains. In particular, while expected inter-correlations between aligned and non-aligned scales would generally be around 0.50 and 0.30, respectively, in this study, they were 0.70 and 0.50, respectively. These results indicate that although scales still captured unique information, their discriminant validity was reduced. This result might be related to the fact that each of the scales was measured in the same way, using parents' reports and that any methodological bias introduced through this approach acts as an amplifier of scale inter-correlations (for extensive discussion on this issue, see Kankaraš et al., 2019).

Assessment scales have shown relatively stable concurrent validity with several essential life markers. Taken together, social and emotional skills accounted for around a quarter of the variation in students' school grades, after a range of demographic and socio-economic variables (age, gender, parental education, household income) of their family were accounted for. Curiosity, persistence and self-efficacy are the strongest predictors of reading, math and science grades, while creativity was the strongest predictor for grades in Arts.

Social and emotional skills, as a whole, accounted for 26% of the observed variation in students' perceived health, after controlling for differences in their socio-economic background. As could be expected, student's energy/enthusiasm scores were the most influential individual predictor of their health among the 19 skill scales. Assessment scales were also strongly related with a range of health-related behaviors, such as brushing teeth (10% of observed variation), eating fruit (12%), doing at least 60 minutes of daily physical activity (15%) or sleeping eight hours or more (8%).

Taken together, although limited in scope due to its non-representative sample, results from this initial study of the assessment scales in the form of parent reports were informative and useful. Scales showed solid psychometric properties, with the observed pattern of relationships with other students' characteristics mainly in line with previous results and theoretical expectations. Importantly, scales were also shown to be relatively easy and fast to administer to this respondent group.

6. Item Trials

———

The Item Trials are a standard phase in the instrument development process in all OECD's assessment studies. As the name suggests, they primarily serve to allow for initial testing of the newly prepared assessment items and scales. Assessment scales implemented in the Item Trials are having a larger number of items than what is planned to be implemented in the Main Study. This is done in order to be able to select the best functioning items based on the empirical evidence from the Item Trials from further rounds of scale construction.

The SSES's Item Trials took place in April and May 2018 in 6 participating sites[5]. In each site, a minimum of 300 students from target populations in each of the two cohorts were selected. Apart from inspecting the psychometric functioning of new assessment items, the Item Trials were an opportunity to examine the newly developed Anchoring Vignettes. Given that this instrument was developed with entirely new content, getting the first empirical results of their psychometric characteristics was especially important.

Although the main focus in item trials was an examination of psychometric characteristics of the assessment scales, this empirical round also involved the implementation of cognitive interviews with parents, teachers, and principals. These interviews were used to check whether parents and teachers understood their respective assessment scales and the newly developed contextual questionnaires for each respondent group.

7.1 Overview of the research stage: Item Trials

7.1.1 Research objectives:

The main goals of the Item Trials were to:

- Select the best functioning items for use in the Field Test and Main Study
- Identify problem items and use gathered psychometric information to remedy them before their subsequent administration in the following phases of the instrument development process.
- Examine how parents, teachers and school principals understood the questions in their assessment scales and contextual questionnaires, i.e., if they were well-formulated and appropriate.
- Investigate psychometric characteristics and functioning of the Anchoring Vignettes.
- Conduct the first round of translations and adaptations of the instruments from their source language (English) to the local languages of participating sites.
- Get insight into the time needed to complete each section of the questionnaires.

7.1.2 Participants

Across the six participating sites, 3,385 students completed questionnaires, with 1823 and 1561 students from the younger and older cohorts, respectively. Among participating students, there were 44% of girls, 52% of boys, and 4% of undeclared.

Cognitive interviews for parents, teachers and school principals were administered in four sites (Ottawa, Istanbul, Moscow, Houston). In total, 52 cognitive interviews were administered across all participating sites, out of which 30 interviews with parents, 20 with teachers and students, and 2 with school principals.

7.1.3 Materials

All students completed 19 assessment scales with 10 and 15 items per scale for the younger and older cohorts, respectively. Older cohorts' scales had the same ten items as the younger cohort scales, plus an additional five items. Students also completed a full set of 15 anchoring vignettes.

Parents and teachers were asked to evaluate their versions of the assessment scales and contextual questionnaires. Assessment scales for parents consisted of the same ten items as those for the younger cohort, while scales for teachers consisted of a subset of 3 items from these scales. School principals were only evaluating their version of contextual questionnaires.

7.1.4 Administration procedures

All student self-report assessment scales were administered online through school-based group administration. The conditions were similar to those used in the Field Test and the Main Study. Administration time was, on average, around 35 minutes for the older cohort and 25 minutes for the younger cohort (thus, around one minute per 10 questions).

Parent and teacher cognitive interviews were administered either in person or through telephone by trained interviewers. Cognitive interviews were also done with students and school principals in a few cases.

7.1.5 Adaptation and translations of survey instruments

All instruments were adapted and translated into local languages. Specific terms within the source versions of each questionnaire need to be adapted to ensure their applicability in local settings. Examples include names of people or places, or terms relating to countries' education systems, such as the equivalent term for classification of education levels (ISCED).

All source instruments for the study were developed in English. Participating cities where the local language or languages were not English were tasked with translating these instruments. Even participating sites where the primary language of administration is English (Ottawa and Houston) needed to adapt the instruments to ensure that all the items corresponded to their local contexts.

The translation process was comprehensive and involved. In each site, three professional translators were assigned to translate two-thirds of the material, thus ensuring that two independent translators translate each item. After translating two-thirds of the material assigned to them, each translator reviews and provides feedback on the work of the other two translators, and then they discuss in order to reach a consensus on each of the translated items. Then, a local psychometric expert reviews these initial translations, analyzing whether the translation and phrasing for each of the items align with the concepts that they intend to measure and other psychometric considerations. The translated instruments are then sent to the verification contractor (cApStAn) whose linguistic experts review the proposed translations and suggest changes, when necessary. The two parties then discuss any suggested changes and agree on a joint version. This version is then sent to an independent translation referee, who evaluates the translations agreed upon by local translation teams and cApStAn. Translation referees also intervene in cases where an agreement between local teams and cApStAn cannot be reached.

This extensive process of instrument translations was conducted three times during the SSES instrument development process: before the Item Trials, the Field Test and the Main Study. In those cases where items remained the same between these rounds, and items had good psychometric characteristics, local teams used existing translation of the item from the previous round. However, in all other cases where a new or modified item was introduced for the first time in the Main Study, the translation process needed to be organized following the steps outlined.

7.2 Main findings

An in-depth analysis of the Item Trial data has shown satisfactory characteristics of the initial versions of the assessment instruments. Their reliabilities are found to be relatively high already in this early stage, while their validity varied across scales and individual items. In general, instruments had a relatively good ability to distinguish between students with low and high social and emotional skills.

7.2.1 Scale reliabilities

Except for the critical thinking scale, all other scales showed relatively high levels of reliability, with the average Cronbach's alpha of .83 and .87 for scales administered with the younger and older cohorts, respectively. The only exception was the scale measuring critical thinking, which had alpha reliability of only .55 and .69 for younger and older cohort students (see Figure 2). These relatively high levels of archived reliabilities were especially important, given that these scales were to undergo a further reduction in the number of items per scale after this phase. The number of items in a scale is one of the key determinants of scales' reliability, i.e., all other conditions being equal, scales with a higher number of items will be more reliable. Thus, having higher levels of reliability at this stage allowed us to shorten the lengths of the scales while still obtaining satisfactory reliabilities.

Figure 2. Reliability of students' social and emotional skill scales across the two cohorts

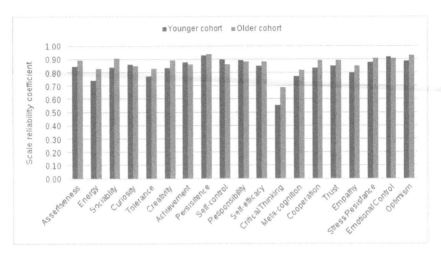

7.2.2 Internal consistency of items

Most correlations between individual items and their scales (an indicator of the degree to which an item fits into the scale) are moderately high (around 0.50). There are, however, a substantive number of items with much lower item-scale correlations. Almost all scales have one or two such items, but some scales were worse in this sense (e.g., scales measuring critical thinking and metacognition), with more than three such items. Also, as could have been expected, more such problematic items were found in scales administered to the younger cohort.

Exploratory Factor Analysis showed one predominant factor in all scales, but the second factor appears in several scales as well. Confirmatory Factor Analysis (CFA) with one factor per scale generally shows good factor loadings across scales. However, a model with an additional "method" factor that accounts for negatively worded items fits better. Such results indicate that students were showing a certain level of response bias. In particular, students showed an agreement bias, a response tendency to agree on positively worded questions and disagree on negatively worded questions, irrespective of the question content. Such response bias is the main reason for including positively and negatively worded items, which allows for statistical control of such tendencies in consequent statistical analyses.

7.2.3 Divergent Validity

Most items have shown relatively good divergent validity with small and insubstantial correlations with other skills scales. However, several items showed small to moderate correlations with other scales of skills from the same skill domain, but also with scales of skills from other skill domains, indicating a potential issue of divergent validity.

At the scale level, scales had moderate correlations with other scales from the same skill domain (0.54). In contrast, their inter-correlations with scales from non-corresponding domains were relatively small (averaging at 0.33). These were much better divergent validities than those obtained from the online study of parents, i.e., there was a lower overlap of captured information by scales measuring different skills and consequently, more unique information provided by each scale. This might be due to the differences in respondents (parents vs. students) and samples (US vs. cities from 6 countries).

7.2.4 Cross-cultural comparability

Cross-cultural comparability of assessment scales was one of the critical aspects of the instrument development process. Given that the Item Trials were implemented in six countries (from four continents) and seven languages, it was possible to conduct an initial examination of the cross-cultural comparability of assessment items and scales as a whole.

Results showed that most items reach so-called metric equivalence, while few also reach scalar equivalence. This meant that at the scale level, the majority of scales reached metric equivalence, with few of them being scalarly equivalent (i.e., fully comparable). Metric equivalence is a comparability level that would allow comparing strengths of structural relationships between skills and other student and contextual characteristics. Since these relationships are the key focus of the SSES survey, achieving metric equivalence is considered as a sufficient level of cross-cultural comparability for the SSES scales.

7.2.5 Anchoring vignettes

The majority of vignettes worked desirably. Vignettes describing persons with a high level of a given skill were mostly receiving high ratings (4 or 5). Likewise, vignettes describing persons with medium skill levels were on average rated 3.5 (slightly biased upwards), while those describing behaviors of a person with lower skill levels were usually rated between 1-2. The only exception to this pattern was a central vignette for the Open-mindedness domain, which seemed to be worded too positively.

There is a moderate degree of difference in responses to anchoring vignettes across sites, indicating that the reference framework students used do differ to a certain degree across different groups.

The variability of factor loadings of assessment items across sites decreased substantially when their responses to anchoring vignettes corrected student responses to assessment items. In particular, average standard deviations of items' factor loadings across sites for all scales dropped from .127 to .092 for the younger cohort and from .111 to .081 for the older cohort. This reduction is an almost 30% drop in this measure of cross-cultural comparability. This result is important since smaller variability in factor loadings leads to better cross-cultural comparability of assessment scales.

7.3 Use of the Item Trials findings

Based on the Item Trial findings and the feedback received from the SSES Technical Advisory Group, assessment instruments were revised and shortened, in preparation for their application in the Field Test. In particular, five items from each of the assessment scales for the older cohort of students were excluded and the best ten items were selected for further scale development. In the case of the scales for younger cohort students, two items from each scale were removed and the remaining eight items were kept for the next stage of instrument development – the Field Test.

The process of item selection was based on several criteria:

- Item-scale correlations (minimum 0.30; the higher, the better)
- Factor loadings (minimum 0.30; the higher, the better)
- Divergent validity – average inter-correlation of an item with other scales (the lower, the better)
- Cross-cultural comparability/differential item functioning (DIF) (preference for items with better cross-cultural comparability)
- Cohort comparability/DIF between students from the two cohorts (preference for items with better cross-cohort comparability)
- Make sure to keep at least one negatively worded item per scale
- Content validity: ensuring that the remaining items are covering the whole breadth of the concept/skill

Using these criteria, we made the selection of 190 items for older cohort students (10 items per scale) as well as 152 items for younger cohort students (8 items per scale). The wording of a few items with identified psychometric issues was slightly modified. The same 152 items used for self-report scales for younger cohort students were prepared for use in the parent-reports in the next phase. Finally, a selection of the best three items in each scale is made for use in the teacher reports (thus, teachers' scales had 57 assessment items in total).

Based on the gathered results, a few vignettes were slightly revised to account for the perceived mismatch between empirical results and their presumed meaning. Feedback obtained from parents, teachers and school principals during cognitive interviews with them was also implemented where appropriate by clarifying certain expressions or adjusting some words and formulations to fit better given respondent group.

7. Field Test

———

The Field Test represents the last phase of the instrument development process before administering the scales in the Main Study. The empirical data obtained during this phase is used to make final adjustments and decisions regarding the content, the form, and the scope of the assessment instruments that will be used in the Main Study. Furthermore, all the SSES' fieldwork and administration procedures are implemented and thoroughly reviewed in this phase before their application in the Main Study.

8.1 Overview of the research stage: Field Test

8.1.1 Objective of the Field Test

The purpose of the Field Test was to check how well all aspects of the study – instruments and administration procedures – operated in the field before the administration of the Main Study in 2019. The Field Test was treated as a general "dress rehearsal" for the Main Study and followed all protocols specified in the SSES Technical Standards and other study documentation.

The main research questions the Field Test is used to answer are:

- Are the assessment instruments reliable and valid?
- Which 15 scales to select for inclusion in the Main Study (out of 19 scales used in the Field Test)?
- Are study design and administration procedures appropriate and efficient?
- What further improvements to the instruments and other aspects of the study need to be implemented to ensure the Main

43

Study meets the intended objectives?

8.1.2 Materials

All study instruments were used in the Field Test. In particular, these consisted of:

- 19 assessment scales for students (self-reports)
- 19 assessment scales for parents (others-reports)
- 19 assessment scales for teachers (others-reports)
- Anchoring vignettes (administered to students, parents and teachers)
- Behavioral indicators (administered to students, parents and teachers)
- Four contextual questionnaires (for students, parents, teachers and school principals)

8.1.3 Participants

A two-stage stratified random sampling model was implemented in the Field Test, which is the same sample design as the one planned for the Main Study. In the first stage, a random sample of schools is selected, followed by the selection of a random sample of individual students within the selected schools.

All ten participating cities took part in the Field Tests[6]. Three sites (Ottawa, Helsinki and Houston) administered the study in two languages due to their local context. The intended sample size for the Field Test was 500 students per site and per cohort. In total, there 13,710 students participated in the survey – 6986 from the younger and 6724 from the older cohort. Students' participation rates were 83% and 79% for younger and older cohort students, respectively. There were 3973 and 3374 parents (participation rates of 50% and 42%). Teacher reports were provided for 6001 and 5693 younger and older cohort students, respectively (participation rates of 73% and 69%).

8.1.4 Administration procedures

The Field Test was administered from 1 October 2018 and until 30 November 2018 (parent and teacher questionnaires were collected until 15 December 2018). Student, teacher and principal questionnaires are administered online. Parent questionnaires are also primarily administered online, but parents in some sites are also offered a paper and pencil option.

Administration of student, teacher and school principal questionnaires is conducted in schools of the selected students. Teachers and school principals were completing their questionnaires individually, on their own time. Students' questionnaires were administered in groups, in classes with selected students from the same cohort.

8.2 Results of the Field Test

8.2.1 Reliability of assessment scales

Figure 3 shows the reliability (Cronbach's alpha) coefficients of students' assessment scales. Overall, the skills have a good reliability, with most of the scales having reliability coefficients between 0.70 and 0.80. In line with the results in previous empirical stages, the scale measuring critical thinking has the lowest reliability coefficients, indicating that there is a problem with the internal consistency of the scale.

Figure 3. Reliability of students' social and emotional skill scales

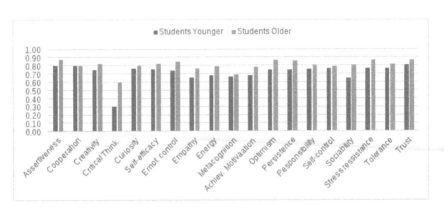

Parents' assessment scales had somewhat lower reliabilities than the scales reported by students with the average at 0.70. As expected, the reliability of the teacher skill scales is the lowest among the three groups of respondents, due to a much lower number of items per scale. In several cases, their reliability is lower than 0.70. Just like with students, critical thinking has the lowest levels of reliability in parent and teacher scales as well. In general, these results show that student and parent reports have satisfactory levels of reliability in most of the scales. At the same time, they indicate that the reliability of some of the teacher scales should be improved.

8.2.2 Validity of skill assessment scales

In order to check scale validities, i.e., whether they measure what they are supposed to measure, we examined scales' relationships with other students' characteristics. We first analyzed correlations between the same skill estimates provided by the three different respondents to see if they are related to one another (convergent validity). We found that the average correlation between how students, parents and teachers have assessed the same students' skill is moderate to substantial across all 19 skills with correlations between 0.30 - 0.50. These results are in line with previous research. They indicate that individual reports from the three respondent groups, apart from shared information, also bring unique aspects that complement one another and broaden the scope of assessment (Kankaraš et al., 2019).

We also examined the divergent validity of the scales by checking whether the assessment scales that are not supposed to be related are indeed uncorrelated. We found that the correlations between estimates of different skills provided by different respondent groups are relatively low (approximately 0.10). However, correlations of the scales from the same respondent groups with other scales were higher and in line with theoretical expectations. Scales measuring skills belonging to the same skill domain (corresponding skills) are found to be more correlated (average correlation of 0.55) than scales measuring skills from different skill domains (non-corresponding skills) – average correlation of 0.35.[7]

Furthermore, we analyzed whether social-demographic background variables and variables that are conceptually relevant (antecedents) for skills have correlations with the skill estimates that are in line with theoretical predictions. Antecedents include, for example, students' gender, school climate and school's extracurricular activities. The results of these analyses are in line with theoretical predictions. For example, boys show slightly higher levels of emotional control and stress resistance than girls, especially in the older cohort. In contrast, girls seem to be more empathetic and co-operative than boys.

Likewise, analysis of relationships between various contextual factors and social and emotional skills offers further indication of the validity of the skill scales. For example, Figure 7 shows that students who report being exposed to bullying in their schools tend to report lower levels of emotional control, stress resistance, cooperation and optimism than other students.

Finally, we also analyzed the correlation between skill estimates and various indicators of student's wellbeing (criterion validity). The study collects information on students' education achievement (grades in math, reading, arts and academic aspiration), active citizenship and civic participation, social connectedness (closeness to family and others), health (healthy behaviors, overall health) and quality of life (subjective wellbeing, life satisfaction and test anxiety). Figure 4 shows the relation between skill estimates from students' assessment scales and the subjective wellbeing of students. In sum, the abovementioned analyses offer strong evidence for the criterion validity of the assessment scales.

Figure 4. Assessment skills related to subjective wellbeing

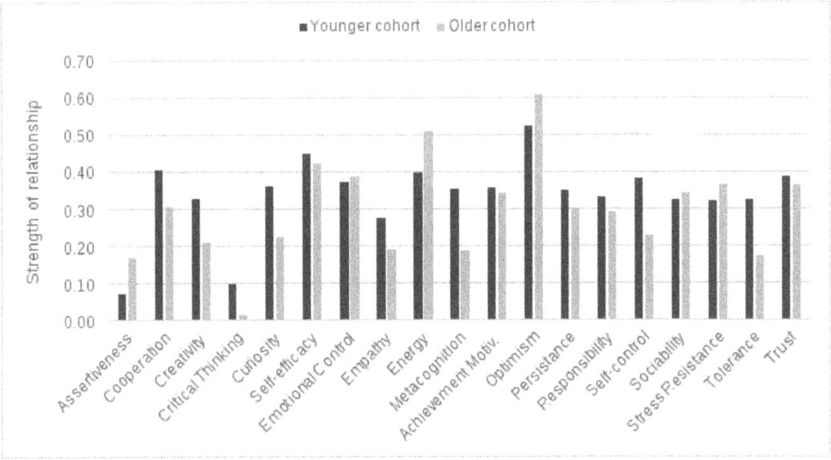

8.2.3 Scale comparability

The findings from the Field Test indicate that the vast majority of assessment items and scales reach metric equivalence but not scalar equivalence. Such results mean that it is possible to compare relationships between skill scales and contextual variables across sites. However, it is not possible to directly compare the averages of the different social and emotional skills across sites. Achieved level of scale cross-cultural comparability would allow sites to go beyond the observation of relations between skills and their antecedents and outcomes in their local context. They would be able to observe the same situation in other participating cities and compare how the same relations vary across these international contexts. These types of comparisons allow for a more comprehensive and in-depth examination of interrelations between relevant aspects and, consequently, for better policy insights.

8.2.4 Anchoring vignettes

There are 15 vignettes per participant, divided into five sets of three vignettes for every domain of the Big Five. The results of the analyses on the anchoring vignettes show that, in general, respondents have understood the vignettes in the intended way by rating higher those vignettes that describe persons with better skills and vice versa (Figure 5).

Figure 5. Average ratings on anchoring vignettes across cohorts

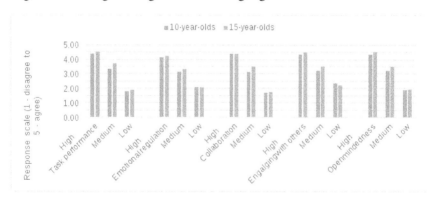

Adjustment of assessment scales based on respondents' answers to anchoring vignettes has shown promising results. In particular, adjusted scales have shown slightly higher reliabilities and cross-cultural comparability (on average, lower item DIF). However, this adjustment also led to the introduction of a common source of variation that leads to undesirable consequences such as higher inter-correlations between scales, i.e., to the decrease of divergent validity of the scales, or inflated reliability coefficients. This is a known issue with the use of anchoring vignettes for correcting answers across multiple scales, at least when these are adjusted using currently recommended approaches.

8.2.5 Behavioral indicators

Results of the analyses of relationships between behavioral indicators and obtained skill estimates of students indicated that most of the behavioral indicators were capturing the intended information. For example, students who don't get into fights (one of the behavioral indicators) tend to have the highest scores on scales measuring emotional control and cooperation. The value of behavioral indicators is not only in providing measures on a set of concrete behaviors of students, that can then be used as indicators of skill development and progress over time. They also provide useful tools for evaluating the construct validity of the assessment scales by providing construct-relevant measures of students' behaviors in various contexts.

8.3 Use of the Field Test findings

8.3.1 Final selection of 15 social and emotional skills that will be assessed in the Main Study

Based on the Field Test findings and other considerations, 15 social and emotional skills were selected for the assessment in the Main Study (see Figure x). Selection criteria, among others, were scale's reliabilities, validities, mutual overlap, analytical and policy value of a scale, cross-cultural comparability, etc. Four scales are excluded from the study at this stage are scales assessing students' critical thinking, meta-cognition, achievement motivation and self-efficacy. In the case of critical thinking and meta-cognition, principal reasons for their exclusion were their weaker psychometric properties. On the other hand, scales assessing achievement motivation and self-efficacy had solid psychometric properties but were largely overlapping with other scales belonging to the skill domain with most skill scales – Task Performance – but also with several other scales. So, it was decided to exclude them from the study as a separate scale but to use the fact that they are closely related to several other scales. In particular, it was decided to construct separate indices from items belonging to other scales that are most closely related to these two scales in the Field Test results. These indices will not be as reliable and valid as separate scales. However, they would still allow for a robust approximation of these two students' skills using results from other available assessment scales.

8.3.2 Final selection of assessment items for the Main Study

Results from the Field Test were also used to reduce further the number of assessment items for the Main Study for the scales of older cohort students, which were reduced from ten to eight items. Item selection criteria were the same used after the Item Trials. The length of scales for younger cohort students and parents remained the same – eight items per scale. Teachers' scales were also kept at three items per scale[8]. Therefore, exclusion of four scales and reduction of the number of items per scale for the older cohort lead to a reduction in the length of assessment scales to the final number of 45 items for teachers and 120 items for other respondent groups.

8.3.3 Anchoring vignettes

Based on the results of the Field Test, it was decided to retain the anchoring vignettes in the Main Study. However, in order to further reduce the response burden of all respondents, it was decided to administer only one set of three vignettes (depicting a high, medium and low-skill person from one of the five domains) per respondent. The five sets with three vignettes each will be randomly assigned across participants thus reducing their response burden from this instrument by 80%.

8.3.4 Behavioral indicators

Based on the Field Test results and to further reduce the response burden of all three groups of respondents, the list of behavioral indicators was reduced from 16 to six behavioral indicators for the younger cohort and from 20 to ten indicators for the older cohort. In addition, out of the 24 indicators used in the Field Test, five were kept for parents and six for teachers (from 20). In the Main Study, each of the behavioral indicators was used only with one group of respondents, i.e., either with students, parents, or teachers.

8. Main Study

———

The Main Study represents a key stage of the SSES intending to gather empirical data used for answering the main research questions of the SSES. All previous empirical rounds in the SSES were used to prepare for the Main Study, ensuring that the instruments used in this round are reliable and valid and that the procedures are appropriate and efficient. The Main Study is administered between October – December 2019 in all ten participating cities, with sample sizes of at least 3,000 students per cohort and per city.

9.1 Overview of the research stage: Main Study

9.1.1 Objective of the Main Study

The purpose of the Main Study was to address the main research questions of the SSES. In particular, its objectives are to:

- Provide participating cities with robust and reliable information on their students' levels of social and emotional skills.
- Provide insights on individual, family, peer and school characteristics that foster or hinder the development of these skills.
- Provide evidence of the predictive value of social and emotional skills for life outcomes in education, conduct, health and personal wellbeing.
- Demonstrate that valid, reliable and comparable datasets on social and emotional skills can be produced across diverse student populations and settings.

9.1.2 Materials

All study instruments were used in the Main Study. These consisted of:

- 15 assessment scales for students (self-reports): 8 items per scale for both cohorts;
- 15 assessment scales for parents (others-reports): 8 items per scale;
- 15 assessment scales for teachers (others-reports): 3 items per scale;
- Anchoring vignettes (administered to students, parents and teachers);
- Behavioral indicators (administered to students, parents and teachers);
- 4 contextual questionnaires (for students, parents, teachers and school principals);

9.1.3 Participants

A two-stage stratified random sampling model was implemented in the Main Study by selecting random samples of schools in the first state and a random sample of individual students from the target populations in the second stage. Selection procedures for the two cohorts were independent from each other.

Ten participating cities took part in the Main Study, but due to the low participation rate of students in Sintra (Portugal), data from this site were not included in the final dataset. Three sites (Ottawa, Helsinki and Houston) administered the study in two languages due to their local context. The target sample size for the Main Study was 3,000 students per site and cohort. In total, 56,743 students across nine sites participated in the Main Study, i.e., on average, 3,152 students per cohort in each site, with 28,818 in the younger and 27,925 in the older cohort. Participation rates of younger and older students were 89.8% and 86.0%.

School participation rates were 96.1% and 95.6% per younger and older cohort. There were 17,940 and 16,423 participating parents (participation rates per eligible student of 56.4% and 50.7%). Teacher reports were provided for 26,381 and 26,302 younger and older cohort students, respectively (response rates per eligible student of 83.2% and 82.9%).

9.1.4 Administration procedures

The Main Study was administered from 1 October 2019 and until 15 December 2019 (parent and teacher questionnaires were collected until 31 December 2019). Student, teacher and principal questionnaires are administered online. Parent questionnaires are also primarily administered online, but parents in some sites are also offered a paper and pencil option.

Administration of student, teacher and school principal questionnaires is conducted in the schools of the selected students. Parents, teachers and school principals were completing their questionnaires individually, at their own time. Students' questionnaires were administered in groups, in classes with selected students from the same cohort.

9.2 Results of the Main Study

The psychometric characteristics and the scaling approach for assessment scales and other methodological details of the Main Study are available in the OECD's Technical Report of the study (OECD, 2021a). It is important to note that due to various psychometric considerations, final scaling of the 15 instruments in the Main Study haven't used all eight items per scale. Instead, the final scale scores were constructed based on a selection of 6 to 7 items per scale (OECD, 2021a).

The results of the Main Study are published in the OECD's report: Beyond Academic Learning: First Results from the Survey of Social and Emotional Skills (OECD, 2021b).

Both reports are freely available at the OECD's library.

9. How to use SSES assessment scales

10.1 Characteristics of the SSES assessment scales

10.1.1 Purpose of the scales

The SSES assessment scales are designed to assess 15 social and emotional skills of students between 10 – 18 years of age.

10.1.2 Structure and content of the scales

The SSES Inventory consists of 45 assessment scales:

- 15 self-report scales for administration with respondents whose skills are being assessed;

- 15 parent-report scales for administration with parents of students whose skills are being assessed;

- 15 teacher-report scales for administration with school teachers of assessed students;

Self-report and parent-report scales consist of eight items/questions (120 items in total), while teacher-reports consist of three items per scale (45 items in total). All three forms of scales used the same response scale with each question having a 5-point Likert response scale ranging from 1 – completely disagree to 5 – Completely agree.

The SSES Inventory assesses the following 15 social and emotional skills, that are grouped into five broader domains:

- Task performance:
    1. Self-control
    2. Responsibility
    3. Persistence
- Emotional regulation:
    1. Stress resistance
    2. Emotional control
    3. Optimism
- Engaging with others:
    1. Energy
    2. Assertiveness
    3. Sociability
- Open-mindedness:
    1. Curiosity
    2. Creativity
    3. Tolerance
- Collaboration:
    1. Empathy
    2. Co-operation
    3. Trust

10.1.3 Administration procedures

Scales are designed for both individual and group administration, either using online or paper-and-pencil formats. In the case of group administration, each respondent has to be able to provide his/her answers individually, without interference from any third party. Standard written instruction has to be provided to each respondent at the beginning of the questionnaire.

The order of questions from different scales is such that a set of 15 consecutive questions has one item from each of the 15 scales.

Administration of the scales is untimed and respondents are allowed to skip individual questions. Self-report and parent-report scales take about 15 minutes to complete (about 1 minute per scale). Teacher-report scales take about 5 minutes to complete.

Target populations

The SSES assessment scales in the form of *self-reports* can be administered to students age 10 or older and the general adult population of any age.

The SSES assessment scales in the form of *other-reports* for parents can be administered to parents of school-age children (age of children between 6 – 18).

The SSES assessment scale in the form of *other-reports* for teachers can be administered to teachers of school-age children (age of children between 6 – 18).

10.2 Other details

10.2.1 How to use the SSES assessment scales

The three forms of assessment scales (students', parents' and teachers' reports) can be used separately or together. The SSES findings indicate strong synergic effects of using all three or at least two of the three forms together (Kankaraš et al., 2019).

When the SSES assessment scales are used in the international context, it is strongly advised to used the SSES Anchoring Vignettes in order to be able to control for possible effects of the reference bias.

Users can administer the scales online or through paper-and-pencil forms. They can use slightly different instructions or administer items in any order. They can also modify the wording of items or remove some items and add items from other scales. Response scales could also be changed. However, any modification of the scales can alter the psychometric properties of the scales, influencing their reliabilities and validities in an unknown way. Researchers are thus encouraged to exercise caution when altering the SSES scales and to implement any changes only when they are sure that the benefits outweigh the risks.

10.2.3 Translations of the SSES scales

The SSES assessment scales are translated into 11 languages: English (source, USA and Canadian versions), Spanish (Columbian, Mexican versions), French (Canadian version), Russian, Chinese (Mandarin), Italian, Portuguese, Finish, Swedish, Korean, and Turkish.

10.2.4 Scoring the SSES scales

There are two types of items in the SSES assessment scales: positively and negatively worded items (they are marked in the scales by signs "+" and "-" respectively). For positively worded items, the response "Completely Disagree" is assigned a value of 1, "Disagree" a value of 2, "Neither Agree nor Disagree" a 3, "Agree" a 4, and "Completely Agree" a value of 5. For negatively worded items, the response "Completely Disagree" is assigned a value of 5, "Disagree" a value of 4, "Neither Agree nor Disagree" a 3, "Agree" a 2, and "Completely Agree" a value of 1.

Assigned numbers can then be used in statistical analyses to calculate scale scores for each respondent. In the SSES scaling was conducted using latent variable models (Item Response Theory and Factor Analytic model). These models allow for better estimation of students' skills than what would be possible by simple calculation of sum-scores or average responses per scale. Furthermore, latent variable models are necessary to investigate the cross-cultural comparability of scale scores.

10.2.5 Scale norms

The SSES scales do not have any norms. This is because it isn't obvious which population and at which time could be regarded as a reference sample. Furthermore, issues such as 'reference bias' or response styles can bias the scores in one population compared to others, thus making any derived 'norms' misleading and detrimental.

We would instead propose the development of "local" norms, that researchers construct themselves based on the results of their research in their specific populations. For example, if one wants to give feedback to a school about their students, they can derive this information by using school-specific average scores and variability ranges. And if they collect information from a school district, then a district-based average score can serve as a meaningful reference point.

Finally, if one is interested in putting their results in a wider national or international context, a researcher can use the published SSES datasets and compare their results with those obtained in the SSES project. However, in doing so researchers need to implement the necessary precautions in comparing the results between groups and samples. In particular, before any comparison takes place they would need to establish measurement invariance between skill estimates from different samples. Depending on the results of these analyses and the established level of measurement invariance, researchers could proceed with substantive interpretations of observed differences of those parameters for which comparability is confirmed. For more details on the issue of cross-cultural and cross-temporal comparability please check the relevant literature (e.g. Kankaraš, 2010).

10. Concluding discussion

The instrument development process for the 45 SSES scales assessing 15 social and emotional skills was complex, involved, and comprehensive. It included more than 150,000 respondents (students, parents and teachers) in six empirical rounds organized in eleven cities worldwide. Fifteen research teams worldwide organized and implemented the process, including more than a thousand project managers, researchers, study administrators, school coordinators, translators, data analysts, coders, quality monitors, and other study officials.

The process started with 380 assessment items and resulted in the best 120 items in their original or slightly modified form. Instrument development utilized quantitative and qualitative methodologies at different stages, gathering complementary insights needed for building reliable and valid scales.

The developed SSES Inventory is used in the SSES Main Study, where it has shown satisfactory psychometric characteristics, reaching relatively high levels of reliability, validity and scale comparability. The instrument functions well in different cultural contexts and, importantly, across different ages of students, starting from the age of ten. Furthermore, the SSES Inventory has shown that its triangulated approach allows for richer information and improvement of the validity of scales based on any of the individual reports (Kankaraš et al., 2019). Thus, the SSES Inventory is shown to be an appropriate and psychometrically solid measure of the social and emotional skills of students aged between 10 – 18 across various cultural contexts. It can be used with any of the three respondent groups individually (students, parents, or teachers), but the best outcomes are obtained when scales are administered to all three respondent groups.

References

Burisch, M. (1984). Approaches to personality inventory construction: A comparison of merits. *American Psychologist, 39*, 214-227.

Chernyshenko, O., Kankaraš, M., & Drasgow, F. (2018). Social and emotional skills for student success and well-being: Conceptual framework for the OECD Study on Social and Emotional Skills. *OECD Education Working Papers.* doi:10.1787/db1d8e59-en.

Connelly, B., & Ones, D. (2010). An other perspective on personality: Meta-analytic integration of observers' accuracy and predictive validity. *Psychological Bulletin, 136*(6), 1092-1122. doi:10.1037/a0021212

De Fruyt, F., Wille, B., & John, O. P. (2015). Employability in the 21st Century: Complex (Interactive) Problem Solving and Other Essential Skills. *Industrial and Organizational Psychology, 8*(2), 276-281.

Duckworth, A. L., Tsukayama, E., & May, H. (2010). Establishing causality using longitudinal hierarchical linear modeling: An illustration predicting achievement from self-control. *Social Psychological and Personality Science, 1*, 311-317. doi:10.1177/1948550609359707

Gosling, S. D., Rentfrow, P. J., & Swann, W. B. (2003). A very brief measure of the Big Five personality domains. *Journal of Research in Personality, 37*(6), 504-528.

Heine, S., Buchtel, E., & Norenzayan, A. (2008). What do cross-national comparisons of personality traits tell us? The case of conscientiousness. *Psychological Science, 19*(4), 309-313. doi:10.1111/j.1467-9280.2008.02085.x

John, O. P., & De Fruyt, F. (2015). *Framework for the Longitudinal Study of Social and Emotional Skills in Cities.* OECD Publishing, Paris.

Kankaraš, M. (2010). *Essays on Measurement Equivalence in Cross-Cultural Survey Research.* Ridderkerk: Ridderprint.

Kankaraš, M. (2017). Personality matters: Relevance and assessment of personality characteristics. *OECD Education Working Papers, 157.* doi:10.1787/8a294376-en

Kankaraš, M., & Suarez-Alvarez, J. (2019). *Assessment Framework of the Study on Social and Emotional Skills.* OECD. Paris: OECD Publishing.

Kankaraš, M., Feron, E., & Renbarger, R. (2019). Assessing students' social and emotional skills through triangulation of assessment methods. *Education Working Paper Series.*

Krosnick, J. A. (1999). Survey research. *Annual Review of Psychology, 50,* 537-567.

Lapsley, D., & Yeager, D. S. (2012). Moral character education. In W. M. Reynolds, G. E. Miller, & L. B. Weiner (Eds.), *Handbook of Psychology: Volume 7 Educational Psychology.* John Wiley and Sons Inc, New Jersey.

National Academy of Sciences. (2012). *Education for Life and Work: Developing Transferable Knowledge and Skills in the 21st Century.* National Academic Press, Washington.

OECD. (2015). *Skills for Social Progress: The Power of Social and Emotional Skills.* OECD Publishing, Paris. doi:10.1787/9789264226159-en

OECD. (2021a). *OECD Survey on Social and Emotional Skills - Technical Report.* Paris: OECD.

OECD. (2021b). *Beyond Academic Learning: First Results from the Survey of Social and Emotional Skills.* Paris: OECD Publishing.

Rammstedt, B., & Kemper, C. (2011). Measurement equivalence of the Big Five: Shedding further light on potential causes of the educational bias. *Journal of Research in Personality, 45*(1), 121-125. doi:10.1016/j.jrp.2010.11.006

Rammstedt, B., Goldberg, L., & Borg, I. (2010). The measurement equivalence of Big-Five factor markers for persons with different levels of education. *Journal of Research in Personality, 44*(1), 53-61. doi:10.1016/j.jrp.2009.10.005

Robins, R. W., Hendin, H. M., & Trzesniewski, K. H. (2001). Measuring global self-esteem: construct validation of a single-item measure and the Rosenberg self-esteem scale. *Personality and Social Psychology Bulletin, 27*(2), 151-161.

Soto, C. J., John, O. P., Gosling, S. D., & Potter, J. (2011). Age differences in personality traits from 10 to 65: Big Five domains and facets in a large cross-sectional sample. *Journal of*

Personality and Social Psychology, 100, 330-348. doi:10.1037/a0021717

Thalmayer, A. G., Saucier, G., & Eigenhuis, A. (2011). Comparative validity of brief to medium-length Big Five and Big Six personality questionnaires. *Psychological Assessment, 23*(4), 995-1009.

Trilling, B., & Fadel, C. (2009). *21st Century Skills: Learning for Life in Our Times.* Jossey-Bass, Francisco.

Varni, J. W., Thissen, D., Stucky, B. D., Liu, Y., Magnus, B., He, J., . . . DeWalt, D. A. (2015). Item-level informant discrepencies between children and their parents on the PROMIS pediatric scales. *Quality of Life Research, 24*, 1921-1937.

Annex: SSES Assessment Scales

List of items

Assertiveness

A leader

Enjoy leading others

Like to be a leader in my class

Want to be in charge

Know how to convince others to do what I want

Dislike leading a team (-)

Like to be the leader of a group

Dominant, and act as a leader

Cooperation

Like to help others

Start arguments with others (-)

Treat others with respect

Get along well with others

Work well with other people

Always willing to help my classmates

Ready to help anybody

Polite, courteous to others

Creativity

Sometimes find a solution other people don't see

Original, come up with new ideas

Have a good imagination

Have difficulty imagining things (-)

Like to create things

Find new ways to do things

Find it difficult to create new things (-)

Have little creativity (-)

Curiosity

Like learning new things

Don't like learning (-)

Love learning new things in school

Like to know how things work

Curious about many different things

Eager to learn

Like to ask questions

Find science interesting

Emotional control

Have unpredictable emotions and moods (-)

Keep my emotions under control

Get mad easily (-)

Know how to control my anger

Change my mood a lot (-)

Not easily upset

Stay calm even in tense situations

Often feel angry (-)

Empathy

Understand what others want

Important to me that my friends are okay

Can sense how others feel

Know how to comfort others

Predict the needs of others

Helpful and unselfish with others

Warm toward others

Rarely ask others how they are feeling (-)

Energy

Full of energy

Have less energy than my classmates (-)

Less active than other people (-)

Show a lot of enthusiasm

Like sports where I can run

Tire out quickly (-)

Slow to start in the morning (-)

Maintain high energy throughout the day

Optimism

Always positive about the future

Enjoy life

A happy person

Often feel sad (-)

Believe good things will happen to me

Look at the bright side of life

Wake up happy almost every day

Expect bad things to happen (-)

Persistence

Keep working on a task until it is finished

Make sure that I finish tasks

Finish what I start

Give up easily (-)

Leave things unfinished (-)

Stop when work becomes too difficult (-)

Hate leaving tasks unfinished

Finish things despite difficulties in the way

Responsibility

Keep my promises

Reliable and can always be counted on

Often forget to do things I promised (-)

Avoid responsibilities (-)

Often forget my duties (-)

A responsible person

Sometimes behave irresponsibly (-)

Forget to do work I was asked to do (-)

Self-control

Say the first thing that comes to my mind (-)

Can control my actions

Think carefully before doing something

Avoid mistakes by working carefully

Careful with what I say to others

Like to make sure there are no mistakes

Stop to think before acting

Often rush into action without thinking (-)

Sociability

Like to spend my free time with others

Have many friends

Make friends easily

Like to be alone (-)

Like talking to a lot of different people

Like to be with my friends

Outgoing and sociable

Have difficulties making friends (-)

Stress resistance

Often feel nervous (-)

Often worried about something (-)

Worry about many things (-)

Afraid of many things (-)

Panic easily (-)

Relaxed and handle stress well

Get nervous easily (-)

Get scared easily (-)

Tolerance

Like hearing about other cultures and religions

Ask questions about other cultures

Love to learn about other countries and cultures

Want to travel to other countries

Feel comfortable in new cultural environments

Not interested in other countries and cultures (-)

Learn a lot from people with differing beliefs

Willing to be friends with people from other cultures

Trust

Think most of my classmates keep their promises

Believe that most people are honest

Believe that my friends will never betray me

Believe most people are kind

Distrust people (-)

Believe that other people will help me

Believe that my friends can keep my secrets

Trust others

Notes:

Items with negative wording (reverse coding) are marked with "(-)"; items should be presented in a random order.

The same 8 items are used for students age 10 or older in form of their self-reports, as well as for parents in the form of other-reports. The first three items from each scale are used in teacher's reports in for of other-reports.

Instructions to respondents

There are three forms of instructions to the respondents, depending whether the scales are administered to students, their parents or teachers.

Instructions in the SSES version for students:

On the following pages you will find a series of statements that may or may not apply to you. There are no right or wrong answers – your own opinion is all that matters. Please answer every statement, even if you are not completely sure of your response.

Please read each statement and select one of the five answers to indicate the extent to which you agree or disagree with that description of you.

(Please select one response in each row.)

Instructions in the SSES version for parents:

On the following pages you will find a series of statements that may or may not apply to you. There are no right or wrong answers – your own opinion is all that matters. Please answer every statement, even if you are not completely sure of your response.

Please read each statement and select one of the five answers to indicate the extent to which you agree or disagree with that description of you.

(Please select one response in each row.)

Instructions in the SSES version for teachers:

On the following pages you will find a series of statements that may or may not apply to this student. There are no right or wrong answers – your own opinion is all that matters. Please answer every statement, even if you are not completely sure of your response.

Please read each statement and select one of the five answers to indicate the extent to which you agree or disagree with that description of you.

(Please select one response in each row.)

Response scale

All scales used a 5-point Likert response scale ranging from "Strongly disagree" to "Strongly agree":

Strongly disagree

Disagree

Neither agree nor disagree

Agree

Strongly agree

---

[1] For fuller examination of the triangulation approach implemented in the Study and its outcomes based on the Field Test data please consult recent publication on the topic (Kankaraš, Feron and Renbarger, 2019).

[2] For full list of TAG experts and the entire organizational structure of the SSES please see Kankaraš and Suarez-Alvarez (2019).

[3] The only difference is in the subject of the sentence. For example, in students' self-reports item is formulated as "I like learning new things", in parents' reports it is formulated as "My child likes learning new things", while in teachers' reports it is formulated as "This student likes learning new things".

[4] https://ipip.ori.org

[5] Item Trials were implemented in Moscow, Houston, Ottawa, Rome, Istanbul and Manizales.

[6] Rome was the eleventh participating city in the Field Test but did not participate in the Main Study.

[7] More information on the validity of the skill estimates can be found in the working paper on Triangulation of assessment methods (Kankaraš et al., 2019).

[8] Although the same number of items per scale is kept for these groups, in few cases actual items were changed in line with the Field Test results.